CRAVE AND COOK

by Virginie Degryse

HOME COOKING DURING THE HOLIDAYS:
RECIPES AND ADVICE FROM A BELGIAN MOTHER
IN A CALIFORNIA KITCHEN.

HOME COOKING DURING THE HOLIDAYS: RECIPES AND ADVICE FROM A BELGIAN MOTHER IN A CALIFORNIA KITCHEN.

WRITTEN BY

Virginie Degryse

FOREWORD
MARTHA ROSE SHULMAN

PHOTOGRAPHY
JOHN MICHAEL RIVA JR.

ART DIRECTION & DESIGN
ALEKSA MARA

Introduction

Breakfast

Starters & Sides

Pea Purée 32

Sweet Corn Purée 32

Cranberry Sauce 37

Assorted Blinis 38

Warm Lima Beans with Pesto 41

Carrot Soufflé 42

Braised Endives 45

Stoemp 46

Cauliflower Gratin 49

Celery Root Purée 51

Chestnut Purée 52

Soups & Salads

Chestnut Mushroom Soup 57

Winter Salad 58

Brussel Sprouts with Lemon 61

Simple Endive Salad 62

Fall Radicchio Salad 63

Turkey & Cranberry Soup 67

Celery Root Soup 71

Entrées (Meat)

Pork Tenderloin 78
Chicken & Nutty Creme Sauce 81
Stuffed Chicken 91

Entrées (Vegetarian)

Pumpkin Risotto 74
Tomato Tartin 82
Winter Vegetable Pot Pie 86

Sweets & Desserts

Cafe Liegois 95
Eggnog Panna Cotta 96
Chocolat Pot du Creme 99
Warm Scandinavian Wine 100
Roasted Apples with Speculoos 103
Poached Pears 105
Orange Nut Cake 106
Eggnog Ice Cream 107
Homemade Eggnog 107

FOREWORD

When I lived in Paris I learned a lot about cooking by watching women like Virginie as they went about their shopping at the street markets in my neighborhood. They were as busy as the next person -- on their way to or from work, dropping off or picking up their kids from school or preschool – but that never seemed to stop them from thinking about making dinner. They always seemed to know what they wanted, to identify what looked good, and to know what nourishing and delicious meals they were going to prepare for their families in under thirty minutes when they got home.

When Virginie moved from Brussels to Los Angeles with her husband and three young children five years ago she brought a passion for cooking along with this innate European know-how. Both blossomed and flourished in the California sunshine. Here she discovered all the produce she had loved at home and more, and all of it with longer growing seasons.

The California bounty made it easy for Virginie to follow her mother's good cooking advice in her new home – to get information from books and recipes, but to add her personal touch and never be afraid to improvise. This is what she does with the healthy, vibrant dishes she publishes on her Crave and Cook blog, made without fuss and irresistible to kids and adults alike.

But in November, even under the blue skies of an 80-degree afternoon, Virginie becomes nostalgic about the cooler-weather recipes that go hand in hand with the holiday season in her native Belgium. She craves the chestnuts that every child (and adult) in Europe looks forward to in December, root vegetables like céleriac that she mashes with potatoes, and cold weather chicories like endive and radicchio.

When Virginie craves something, she cooks. She braises her endives, and as her mother used to do to sweeten their bitter edge, caramelizes them with a little sugar. She tosses radicchio with sweet pears and inter vegetables into potpies with buttery puff pastry lids, and crumbles the Belgian spice cookies (called Speculoos) that she loves over baked apples. She serves festive blinis with assorted toppings on Christmas Eve, and makes an indulgent Christmas morning French toast casserole with challah, soaked overnight in a mixture of eggs and eggnog, then baked until golden while she and her family are opening their presents, a wonderful holiday twist that goes right to the heart of her mother's advice – "never be afraid to improvise."

Virginie knows how to simplify preparations so that even a complex dish is easily accomplished in minimal time. This is one reason why her holiday recipes are so appealing: they are doable. She knows when it's okay to use store-bought ingredients. Why not use good packaged puff pastry for winter vegetable potpies and put the time and effort into assuring that the filling is delicious. No need to make the blinis if you can find good ones in the supermarket; the focus here is on the toppings.

A wonderful chestnut soup or puree is easy to accomplish with a good jar of chestnuts. The comforting recipes in Virginie's Crave and Cook Holiday Cookbook are inspired by old and new world ingredients and traditions, a touch of Europe warmed by the California sun. Like Virginie, they bring together the best of both worlds.

MARTHA ROSE SHULMAN
Cookbook Author &
New York Times Contributor

Brussels, Belgium

INTRODUCTION

For as long as I can remember, cooking has always been an important part of my life. I started baking with my mother after school when I was just a little girl. We would make chocolate cakes, chocolate truffles, strawberry shortcakes. Once I was hooked to baking, she started to teach me my way around the kitchen. She used to tell me to get inspiration from books but to always add your personal touch and never be afraid to improvise.

Through the years, I've continued cooking what I love and sharing it with my closest loved ones; my husband and my children. For me, family and cooking are profoundly linked and my greatest pleasure is to cook for them. Having dinner together as a family is the perfect time to bond and check in on one another, to make sure everyone is all right. To even have the time to ask, how was your day?

When I cook for my family I try to be mindful of everyone's different taste while making sure to provide the opportunity of getting out of their comfort zone. Trying to teach my kids to be adventurous and open to new cuisine and flavor variety is a driving force for me.

A few years ago, we moved from Belgium to Los Angeles. With Whole Foods, farmer markets and fresh organic produce everywhere we turn, the local resources in this city are truly inspiring. I have always loved to cook ingredients as they are, to leave them true to their character and try not cover them with too much spices or sauces. Moving to California has pushed me even more in that direction.

The winter flavors and Holiday dishes are my favorite. They take me back to my childhood and I am flooded with memories of family gatherings when I was a little girl. We had a routine: We would all share a house by the seaside for Christmas and New Year. My grandma would be cooking with my mom and my aunts. My cousins, brother and I would be running all over the place having a blast. All of us kids slept in the same room where we shared stories over laughter at night when we should have been asleep. We would have a delicious dinner for Christmas Eve and then go to midnight mass. The next day, when we woke up to all the presents Santa had brought us, there would be crepes and hot chocolate with whipped cream for breakfast with Christmas carols in the background. The joy was always amplified by the food.

I keep these memories in mind when I prepare Holiday meals today. What are the new traditions of the Holidays now that we live in California? How can I merge them with my old memories to provide them with the same sensations I once had as a child?

I always play Christmas songs in the background as soon as November begins. I also have Holiday scented candles burning around the house, start making eggnog and even roasted chestnuts. The wood-burning fire cracks in the chimney, creating a cozy winter atmosphere and amazing wood burning smell. And, well, I cook!

Cooking can be scary and some people find it inaccessible. Especially during the Holidays where cooking is a part of the traditions, where you are serving more people than usual, and you're not making your ordinary dinners! Through this book, I try to demystify Holiday cooking while showing you that delicious food can be prepared without a culinary degree or professional background. Sharing what I cook makes me as happy as showing how simple, enjoyable, and quick it can be. The more festive your table is, the easier it is to feel that sensation of Holiday joy.

I want to dedicate this book to my amazing kids and husband who inspire me everyday and appreciate everything I do and cook for them. Thanks to them, I feel inspired more and more and always try to come up with new dishes and flavors. Thank you, for always being adventurous and for always being up for whatever I present you with.

AND WITH THAT, BON APPETIT!

Virginie Degryse

For my Family

PETIT DÉJEUNER (BREAKFAST)

Warm Apple Pie Oatmeal

Pumpkin Spice Oatmeal

Savory Buckwheat Crêpes

Pumpkin French Toast

Pain Perdu

PORRIDGE AUX POMMES
(WARM APPLE PIE OATMEAL)
SERVES 4

This is a perfect breakfast for Christmas morning, not just because of the warm smell of apple and cinnamon this will fill your house with, but because you can prepare it the night before and heat it up in the morning in no time. The almond milk gives the porridge a smooth consistency.

1 cup rolled oats

2 large apples, peeled and chopped into 1/2-inch pieces

2 tsp ground cinnamon

A pinch of fine sea salt

1 1/2 cups water

1/2 cup almond milk

2 tbsp pure maple syrup

1/2 cup unsweetened applesauce

1/2 tsp pure vanilla extract

1. Place the oats, apple, cinnamon, salt, water, maple syrup, and applesauce in a medium saucepan over medium heat and stire together. Bring to a simmer and cook, stirring often, until the mixture thickens and the oats are soft, about 9 to 15 minutes.

2. Stir the pure vanilla extract and almond milk into the warm oatmeal and combine well.

3. Pour into bowls and serve with your desired toppings.

tip
I love adding a crunch to oatmeal, and suggest sprinkling chopped nuts, chopped fresh apples, or granola on top.

FLOCONS D'AVOINE AU POTIRON
(PUMPKIN OATMEAL)
SERVES 4

There's something so perfect about winter mornings paired with a warm cup of homemade porridge. I'm a big fan of oatmeal because its naturally healthy, and with extra pumpkin laying around in the fall, this flavorful pumpkin oatmeal sets the tone for the day.

1 cup rolled oats

2 tsp ground cinnamon

1 tsp of allspice

Pinch fine sea salt

1 1/2 cups water.

1/2 cup of almond milk

2 tbsp pure maple syrup

1 cup of pumpkin purée

1/2 tsp pure vanilla extract

1. In a medium sized pot over medium heat, whisk together the oats, pumpkin pie, cinnamon, allspice, salt, water and maple syrup until combined.

2. Cook over medium heat for about 9 to 15 minutes, stirring often.

3. When the mixture thickens and the oats soften, it is ready.

4. While it's warm, stir in the pure vanilla extract and almond milk.

Pour into bowls and serve with your desired toppings.

tip

Just like the apple oatmeal, this can be prepared the evening before as well.

CRÊPES SALÉES
(Savory Buckwheat Crêpes)
Serves 4-6

I love this recipe for Christmas brunch! Crêpes can be scary the first time you make them (I mess them up every once in a while) and it is ok. You just prepare extra batter and start over. The buckwheat flour is the surprising ingredient here, giving it a savory and wholesome flavor regular flour crêpes just don't have. That being said, you can easily swap out the buckwheat flour for regular all-purpose flour if the idea of buckwheat scares you, or if you just don't have any in your cabinet. This is a recipe where toppings improvisation is fun, whatever you have at hand and like… You can even have it is a buffet and let you family and friends help themselves.

1 cup of buckwheat flour

1 1/2 cup of milk

2 large eggs

1 pinch of salt

Toppings: cheese, eggs, tomatoes, cooked spinach, mushrooms, and any other leftovers you may have from Chistmas dinner.

1. Put everything in the blender and process until smooth.

2. Pour 1/4 cup in a 9 inch hot and greased pan and distribute the batter evenly in the pan.

3. Cook for a few minutes and flip over. Keep on going until you run out of batter. Keep them warm until ready to serve.

tip

The batter can be prepared in advance and refrigerated for a few days. To save even more time, you can also cook the crêpes in advance and even freeze them, warm them up, and serve.

PAIN PERDU AU POTIRON
(Pumpkin French Toast Casserole)
Serves 8

The eggnog french toast casserole is such a hit in my family that I decided to try new flavors and experiment and see what else I could come up with. I love pumpkin waffles and pumpkin pancakes so why not pumpkin french toast casserole. The pumpkin version is my favorite of the 2 but the eggnog is still number 1 for my husband and kids. It doesn't matter which one I make - there are never any leftovers!

6 eggs

1 tsp vanilla extract

2 tsp ground cinnamon

1/2 tsp ground cloves

1/4 tsp ground nutmeg

1 tbsp maple syrup

1 (15 ounce) can pumpkin purée

1 loaf challah bread, cut in cubes

For the toppings

1/3 cup brown sugar

1/4 tsp ground cinnamon

2 tbsp all-purpose flour

1 tbsp butter, softened

1/2 cup of mixed nuts, chopped

1. Grease a baking dish with butter

2. In a bowl, whisk together the eggs, vanilla, cinnamon, cloves, nutmeg and maple syrup.

3. Beat the pumpkin in until fully incorporated.

4. Arrange the bread cubes in a single layer in the prepared baking dish.

5. Pour the pumpkin mixture over the bread cubes, and gently toss to coat. Place in the fridge and leave overnight.

6. Preheat your oven to 375

7. Stir together the topping ingredients with a fork in a small bowl until the mixture is crumbly, and sprinkle over the bread cubes.

8. Bake until the top of the casserole is golden brown, 30-40 minutes.

tip
Warm up the maple syrup before serving and it will bring out the flavor even more!

PAIN PERDU
(Eggnog French Toast Casserole)
Serves 4-6

This is one of my family's all time favorites! I had fun experimenting more this year and came up with a pumpkin version, which taste just as delicious as this one.

2 tbsp maple syrup

1 load challah bread, cut into 1-inch cubes

1 tbsp Cinnamon

1 tsp Nutmeg

6 eggs

2 cups prepared eggnog

1 tsp vanilla

1 pinch of salt

For the sauce

2 persimmons chopped

2 tbsp orange

1tsp orange zest

1-2 tsp of maple syrup (star with one, and add if necessary)

Put everything in a pot, bring to boil and lower to simmer for 15 minutes

1. Grease a baking dish with butter or coat with nonstick cooking spray.

2. In a large bowl, whisk the eggs and mix in the eggnog and vanilla and all the spices.

3. Evenly pour this custard mixture over the bread cubes. Press down lightly on the bread to make sure it's all coated/soaked.

4. Tightly cover baking dish with aluminum foil and refrigerate overnight, at least 8 hours.

5. Remove the baking dish from the refrigerator. Bake at 325°F, covered, for 40 minutes.

6. Increase oven temperature to 375°F and remove foil.

7. Bake, uncovered, for an additional 5 to 10 minutes or until knife inserted in center of casserole is clean (and mostly dry) and top is puffy and golden brown.

6. Add sliced almonds, fresh blueberries (or other fresh berries) and sprinkle some powder sugar.

tip

You can prepare all the wet ingredients in a tight jar and keep it in the fridge for 2-3 days. Just mix it up when ready to use.

You can also decide to prepare this recipe not as a casserole but as a traditional way of preparing french toasts by dipping bread in the mixture and cooking right away

POUR COMMENCER ET ACCOMPAGNER (STARTERS & SIDES)

Pea Purée

Sweet Corn Purée

Cranberry Sauce

Assorted Blinis

Warm Lima Beans with Pesto

Carrot Soufflé

Braised Endives

Stoemp

Cauliflower Gratin

Celery Root Purée

Chestnut Purée

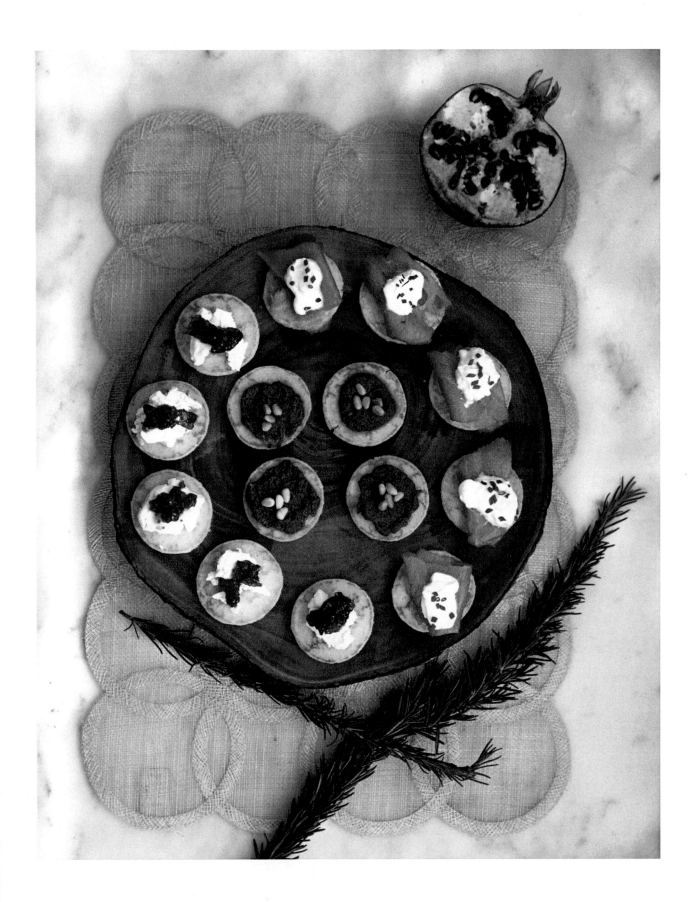

PURÉE DE PETITS POIS
(PEA PURÉE)

I like this purée and the corn purée that follows it because the recipes don't call for potatoes. The purées are lighter than traditional purées, but they still have the same smooth, silky consistency.

2 tbsp olive oil	1 to 2 tbsp butter
1 shallot, minced	1 cup chicken stock
4 cups peas (fresh or frozen)	salt & pepper

1. Heat the olive oil over medium heat in a large skillet or saucepan and sautée the shallot for a couple of minutes, until tender and translucent.

2. Add the peas and continue cooking for a few minutes.

3. Add the stock, bring to a simmer and simmer uncovered for 5 minutes.

4. Transfer the peas with some of the liquid to a food processor, add 1 tbsp butter, salt & pepper, and process for 2 minutes.

5. Taste, adjust seasoning, and check the consistency. If too thick, add more stock and the other tbsp of butter if desired.

PURÉE DE MAÏS
(SWEET CORN PURÉE)

2 tbsp olive oil	1-2 cup chicken stock
4 cups frozen corn kernels	1 to 2 tbsp butter
1 shallot, minced	salt & pepper

1. Heat the olive oil over medium heat in a large skillet or saucepan and sautée the shallot for a couple of minutes, until tender and translucent.

2. Add the corn and continue cooking for a few minutes, until the corn is tender.

3. Add the stock, bring to a simmer and simmer uncovered for 5 minutes.

4. Transfer the corn with some of the liquid to a food processor, add 1 tbsp butter, salt & pepper, process for 2 minutes.

5. Taste, adjust seasoning, and check the consistency. If too thick, add more stock and the other tbsp of butter if desired.

SAUCE AUX AIRELLES
(CRANBERRY SAUCE WITH APPLE & GINGER)
SERVES 6

Cranberry sauce makes so many holiday dishes feel complete. I have always loved the tanginess and sweetness it adds to turkey, chicken, or even pheasant. Store bought cranberry sauce is good, but nothing beats the taste of homemade cranberry sauce in the holiday season.

1/2 cup granulated sugar

1 cup orange juice

1 lb fresh cranberries, washed

2 apples, peeled and sliced

1/4 tsp ground cinnamon

1/2 tsp ground ginger

1. In a sauce pan, combine the orange juice, sugar, cinnamon and ginger and heat up the mixture until the sugar is dissolved, around 5 minutes.

2. Add the cranberries, cover and bring to a boil. Lower the heat and let simmer for 10 minutes.

3. Add the apples and cook for an additional 5 minutes.

4. Transfer to a bowl and let it cool to serve.

tip

Try replacing coconut sugar, date sugar, or maple syrup for the granulated sugar.

If you don't have fresh cranberries, you can make this recipe using frozen cranberries, thawed.

HORS D'OEUVRE
(Blinis with Assorted Toppings)
Serves 6

Blinis remind me of Christmas Eve because it was the one time a year when we would eat caviar. My mom would spread creme fraiche over blinis and top it with caviar. Just thinking of this makes me smile and get hungry! I thought it would be fun to come up with different versions of blinis that would be great for the entire family. Here are my family's top 3 to get you started, but feel free to experiment with other yummy combinations.

2 packs of blinis (you can find them in the freezer section at most grocery store)

un	deux	troix
smoked salmon	goat cheese	pesto
Greek yogurt	fig jam	pine nuts
chopped chives		

1. Top blinis with a piece of salmon and a dollop of yogurt. Sprinkle with chives.

2. Spread a spoonful of goat cheese over the blinis and top the goat cheese with a small spoonful of fig jam.

3. Spread a spoonful of pesto over the blinis and sprinkle a couple of pine nuts on top.

tip
I recommend heating up the blinis in a medium oven for a couple of minutes. You can eat them cold, but they taste much better warm.
Buy extra bilinis and keep them in your freezer for the next bilini occasion.

FÈVES AU PESTO
(WARM LIMA BEANS WITH PESTO)
SERVES 4-5

This is a super easy dish that impresses with its unique flavors. The best part is, it will work with canned beans and store bought pesto. All you need is a fresh lemon and a stove top.

1 can lima beans

1 tbsp olive oil

3-4 tbsp pesto

1-2 tbsp fresh lemon juice

salt & pepper

1. Heat the lima beans and olive oil in a medium saucepan over medium heat.

2. Add the pesto and lemon juice.

3. Season to taste with salt & pepper and serve warm.

tip

If you don't have lima beans, try this dish with canned white beans, or canned chickpeas.

SOUFFLÉ AUX CAROTTES
(Carrot Soufflé)
Serves 6

One of the first things I learned from my Mom was how to make chocolate soufflé, which to this day remains one of my favorite desserts. Perfecting a soufflé can be quite a feat, yet my Mom had tricks to avoid disaster, which made her a Superwoman in my eyes.

Through the years I have tried many different variations of this easy dish, which is part carrot cake, part soufflé, and very quick to make. It has a light, fluffy texture but also some texture, so all of your tastebuds will be happy. For the nicest presentation use individual dishes.

1lb carrots, cooked and mashed

1/2 cup of granulated sugar (can substitute coconut sugar, date sugar or maple syrup)

1 teaspoon baking powder

1/2 cup butter, softened but not warm or melted

3 eggs, beaten

3 tablespoons all-purpose flour

1 teaspoon pure vanilla extract

1 teaspoon cinnamon (or to taste)

1/2 teaspoon freshly grated nutmeg (or to taste)

1. Preheat oven to 350 degrees F and grease one 2-quart baking or soufflé dish or six individual dishes.

2. Mix all of the ingredients in a bowl with a mixer. Scrape into the prepared baking dish or dishes.

3. Bake 40-50 minutes if baking in one dish, 20-30 minutes if baking in smaller ramekins, until a knife comes clean. Serve hot or cold. It is delicious either way and is even delicious reheated the next day.

tip

If you want to mix it up, you can easily substitute the carrots for sweet potatoes, butternut squash, and even pumpkins. You can even try a combination of any two for a broader flavor.

43

CHICONS CARAMÉLISÉS
(Braised Endives)
Serves 6

Endives are good braised, raw, and steamed. Here is a super-easy version of braised endives with intriguing flavors. The dish is sweet and bitter at the same time, which makes it not only delicious but also kid-friendly.

2 lbs endives, cut in half lengthwise.
1 tbsp grapeseed oil
2 garlic cloves, minced
1/2 cup sugar
salt & pepper

1. Quickly rinse the endives and pat dry with a paper towel. Do not soak them!

2. Heat the oil and garlic together in a large skillet and sauté the garlic for 2 minutes.

3. Add the endives to the skillet, face down, and sprinkle on 3 tablespoons of the sugar, some salt, and pepper.

4. Add 1 to 2 tbsp water to the pan (this will help the veggies to steam) cover and cook over medium heat for10 minutes.

5. Uncover, turn the endives face up, sprinkle with another 3 tablespoons sugar, season with salt and pepper, cover and cook for another ten minutes, until the endives are tender all the way through.

6. When the endives are cooked, uncover, add the remaining sugar and raise the heat to high.

7. Once the sugar is caramalized, the endives are ready to be served.

tip
You can substitute coconut sugar, date sugar or even maple syrup for the granulated sugar.

STOEMP
(VEGGIE AND POTATO MASH)
SERVES 6

This mix of vegetables mashed with potatoes is a Belgian classic called Stoemp (pronounced *Stoomp*). Stoemp has endless variations. Popular choices to use in this mash are carrots, spinach, broccoli, leeks, corn, peas, and endives. But my personal favorite is made with leeks.

5 large potatoes, peeled and chopped in cubes

salt & pepper

pinch of freshly grated nutmeg

1 small onion, sliced

2 garlic cloves, minced

4 medium leeks, finely sliced

1 tbsp olive oil

4 tbsp butter

1/4 cup of half & half

1/2 cup vegetable stock

1. Cook the potatoes until easily pierced with knife, nice and tender. Drain.

2. Mash the potatoes with a fork and add salt, pepper and nutmeg.

3. While the potatoes are cooking, slice up the leeks, onions and garlic and lightly sauté them in a small saucepan in the olive oil until just tender.

4. Add the half & half and stock. Simmer for approximately 5-8 minutes, until very tender. Remove from the heat and stir this vegetable goodness to the mashed potatoes.

Tip

When mashing the ingredients together, leave big chunks of veggies to create lots of flavor. Try substituting sweet potatoes for the regular potatoes for a sweeter mash.

GRATIN DE CHOU-FLEUR AU FROMAGE DE CHÈVRE
(CAULIFLOWER AND GOAT CHEESE GRATIN)
SERVES 4-6

I love gratins around the holidays, especially when the weather is cold, but I have issues with how complicated or heavy with cheese these dishes can be. I've lightened this gratin by substituting chicken stock for some of the cream. The goat cheese gives it an interesting twist.

1 head cauliflower, cut into florets

1 cup heavy cream

1 cup chicken stock

2 cups grated Parmesan

6 oz. goat cheese, cut into small pieces

1 tsp freshly grated nutmeg

salt & pepper

1. Preheat oven to 400 degrees F.

2. Mix together the stock, heavy cream, salt and paper and nutmeg.

3. Layer the cauliflower and the cheeses in a medium-sized casserole dish and pour in the cream and stock mix.

4. Bake for 20 to 30 minutes, or until the cauliflower is soft and the sauce has thickened slightly. Remove from the oven and let rest for 10 minutes before serving.

tip
Wash the cauliflower in advance and store it in the fridge.

PURÉE DE CÉLÉRI
(CELERY ROOT PURÉE)
SERVES 6

I love the earthy flavor of celery root. To me, root vegetables like these are the essence of fall and winter.

2 large celery roots (about 2 1/2 pounds total), trimmed, peeled and cut into 2-inch cubes

1 medium russet potato (about 10 ounces), peeled and cut into 2-inch cubes

1 small onion, peeled and quartered

3 tbsp butter, cut into pieces

1 tbsp salt for the cooking water, plus more to taste

White pepper to taste

Milk as desired (optional)

1/2 tsp freshly grated nutmeg

1. Fill a large pot of water, salt generously and add the celery root cubes, potato cubes, and onion quarters. Bring to boil.

2. Reduce heat to medium and simmer until vegetables are tender, about 30 minutes.

3. Drain and discard cooking liquid.

4. Put vegetables and butter through a ricer or a food mill, or use a processor to purée until smooth. Stir in some milk if you want it smoother. Season to taste with salt, white pepper and nutmeg.

tip
This flavor of this purée pairs perfectly with the *poulet en robe d'auomne* (pg. 76).
This dis is creamy without the help of cream or milk as celery root is a watery vegetable, but feel free to add 1 or 2 tablespoons of each for extra creaminess.

PURÉE DE MARRONS
(CHESTNUT PURÉE)
SERVES 6

This smooth and creamy chestnut purée goes just as well on chicken as it does on its own. A bowl of this at your table is sure to be a hit. I love it so much, I can eat it on its own, as a side, or even as a dessert as it has a certain sweetness to it! It is sure to be a hit.

1lb jarred cooked chestnuts
2 large yukon gold potatoes
1/2 cup half & half
2 tbsp butter, at room temperature
salt & pepper
1/4 tsp freshly grated nutmeg

1. Place the potatoes in a saucepan, cover with water, salt generously and bring to a boil. Reduce heat to medium and boil the potatoes until soft, about 15 minutes.
2. While the potatoes are cooking, bring a saucepan of water to a boil, add the chestnuts, reduce the heat and simmer until they soften, about 5 minutes. Drain.
3. Place the chestnuts in a bowl and add the cream, salt, pepper and nutmeg. Mash with a fork.
4. Drain the potatoes and add to the chestnuts, along with the butter. The heat of the potatoes will melt the butter. Mash together. You may want to add more cream if the mixture looks too dry. Depending on how you like the consistency, you can either keep mashing with a fork or use a submersion blender to make the puree completely smooth.

5. Season to taste with salt, pepper and nutmeg.

tip
Whatever I eat this with, it tastes even better with a drizzle of sauce on it. Try it with the sauce from the chicken or pork.

SOUPES ET SALADES (SOUPS & SALADS)

Chestnut Mushroom Soup

Winter Salad with Cranberries

Brussels Sprouts with Lemon

Simple Endive Salad

Radicchio, Pear & Pomegranate Salad

Turkey & Cranberry Soup

Celery Root Soup

SOUPE DE MARRONS
(Chestnut & Mushroom Soup)
Serves 6

This soup is perfect for colder or rainy days, which are numerous in Belgium. It is comforting, creamy without the use of cream, and has a sweetness to it that just does it for me. Enjoy it by the fireplace on a cold evening!

2 tbsp olive oil

1 small onion, chopped

1 garlic clove, minced

6 oz. cremini mushrooms

2 oz. shiitake mushrooms, stems removed

1 lb chestnuts (I used jarred chestnuts)

6-8 sprigs fresh thyme

6 cups chicken stock

Chopped chestnuts and Greek yogurt for garnish (optional)

1. In a large, heavy soup pot or saucepan, heat the oil over medium heat and add the onion and garlic. Sauté for 1 minute.

2. Add the mushrooms and sauté for 5-7 minutes, stirring often, to release their flavor.

3. Add the chestnuts and thyme and stir together gently for another 2 minutes.

4. Add the stock, bring to boil, reduce the heat, cover and simmer for 1 hour.

5. Transfer, in batches, to a food processor, add salt and pepper, and process until smooth. Taste and adjust seasonings.

6. Garnish each serving with chopped chestnuts on top and a dollop of Greek yogurt.

Tip
Use vegetable stock to make this soup completely vegan!

SALADE D'HIVER AUX AIRELLES
(WINTER SALAD WITH ROASTED BUTTERNUT SQUASH AND CRANBERRY DRESSING)
SERVES 6

This salad, with its tangy, sweet, flavorful cranberry dressing, takes you right to the holidays. I designed it to go with thanksgiving dinner - stuffing, cranberries, and of course, turkey.

1/2 butternut squash, peeled and cut into cubes
1 to 2 tablespoons olive oil, as needed
Salt & pepper
1 head butter lettuce washed and dried
1 cup pumpkin seeds
1/2 cup raisins or dried cranberries

For the dressing
2 tbsp cranberry juice
1 tbsp of red wine vinegar
1/2 cup of good olive oil
salt & pepper

1. Preheat the oven to 400 degrees F. Rub the butternut squash with olive oil, season with salt and pepper and place on a baking sheet. Roast for 20 minutes or until tender, stirring halfway through.
2. Meanwhile, make the dressing by simply whisking the ingredients together.
3. Combine the lettuce, pumpkin seeds, raisins or dried cranberries and warm butternut squash in a bowl.
4. Add the dressing, toss well, and serve.

Tip
You can customize this salad with any number of items. Top with different varieties of nuts, toasted quinoa, roasted sweet potatoes, chestnuts... the list is endless. The salad is naturally vegan, but to increase protein you can add chicken or turkey.

CHOUX DE BRUXELLES AU CITRON ET NOIX
(Brussel Sprouts with Lemon and Walnuts)
Serves 6

Growing up, just hearing the words "brussel sprouts" would make us tremble. We viewed them as the ultimate punishment, as they were always so bitter and mushy. Then one day when I was in my 30's I went to a dinner party where they served Brussel sprouts. I didn't to be rude to our hostess so had no choice but to go for it, and was so impressed by the way the vegetable had been transformed into something I enjoyed. Since then I have explored every way to prepare this surprising veggie: raw or cooked, hot or cold. This dish is so simple and delicious, it will surprise you and everyone sitting at your Christmas table, especially those who feel the same way that I used to about Brussels sprouts.

2 lb. brussels sprouts, stem ends trimmed, cut in half

1-2 tbsp olive oil

Coarse salt and freshly ground pepper

2 tsp freshly squeezed lemon juice

1/2 cup walnuts, toasted and coarsely chopped

1. Preheat the oven to 400 degrees F.

2. Place the brussels sprouts on a baking sheet and toss with the olive oil, salt and pepper.

3. Place in the oven and roast for approximately 15-20 minutes, until crispy brown, stirring half way

through.

4. When ready add the lemon and walnuts, toss and enjoy!

Tip

This preparation can be made with green beans, broccoli or even cauliflower.

SALADE D'ENDIVES
(Simple Endives Salad)
Serves 5

Endives are originally from Belgium. Raw, braised or steamed, I think I have had them all. This salad is crisp and fresh and will be a nice side with your holiday meals.

4 endives, sliced

1 apple, peeled and cut in cubes

3 oz. goat cheese

1/2 cup walnuts

For the dressing

1 tbsp dijon mustard

1 tbsp apple cider vinegar

1/2 cup olive oil

salt to taste

1. In a small bowl, whisk together the mustard, apple cider vinegar, and olive oil. Season to taste with salt.
2. Assemble the salad in a serving bowl.
3. Add the dressing and toss to combine.

tip
Feel free to play around with toppings. You can add pears instead of apples, replace the goat cheese with blue cheese or gouda, skip the walnuts and add almonds or pepitas.

SALADE D'AUTOMNE AU RADICCHIO
(Radicchio Salad)
Serves 5

The bitterness of the radicchio in this salad is beautifully offset by the sweet pears and pomegranate. Manchego cheese and walnuts add warmth and complete the salad in a perfect way.

1 radicchio, washed and leaves separated (or simply chopped)

2-3 bunches either arugula or baby spinach (delicious with both)

1 pear, washed and cut into small cubes

1 cup pomegranate seeds

1/2 cup shaved manchego (use a vegetable peeler)

1/2 cup walnuts (optional)

For the dressing

1-2 tbsp dijon mustard

1-2 tbsp apple cider vinegar

3/4 cup olive oil

1. Combine the radiccio, arugula or baby spinach, pear and pomegranate seeds in a serving bowl or on large platter. Sprinkle the manchego and walnuts over the top.
2. Place all of the dressing ingredients in a jar and shake well.
3. Drizzle the dressing over the salad, and serve

tip

This salad calls for variety, so when you feel like you have had it enough times you can vary the ingredients. Change the cheese, add dried cranberries, replace the walnuts with another nut - or even better toast the walnuts!

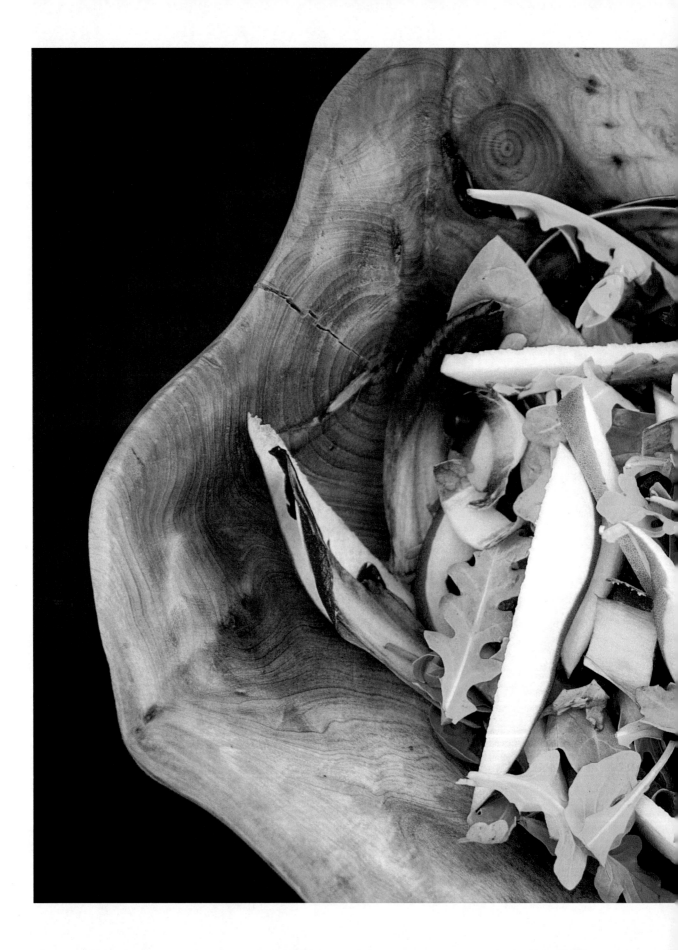

SOUPE A LA DINDE AUX AIRELLES
(TURKEY & CRANBERRY SOUP)
SERVES 4-6

In Europe, we often start meals with soup. This one is extremely comforting and surprisingly light. It makes an excellent meal-starter and one that will please
any group of happy eaters.

4 tbsp grape seed oil

1 onion, peeled and chopped

1 celery stalk, chopped

2 garlic, minced

2 carrots, sliced

1 parsnip, peeled and cut into cubes

1 large potato (or sweet potatoes), peeled and cut into cubes

1 turkey breast

1/2 cup fresh cranberries

1 orange, zested and juiced

4 cups turkey or chicken stock

1 sprig fresh rosemary

1 sprig thyme

1/2 cup brussels sprouts, trimmed and chopped

1. Heat the oil over medium heat in a large, heavy skillet and sauté the carrots, onions, celery, parsnips, and potatoes for 8-10 minutes.

2. Add the turkey and brown for an additional 5 minutes.

3. Meanwhile, in a small saucepan combine the cranberries and the orange juice and simmer for 5-10 minutes.

4. Add the stock, rosemary and thyme to the turkey and vegetables and bring to a boil.

5. Add the brussel sprouts and half of the cranberry mix. Cook for 10 minutes, or until the turkey is cooked through.

6. When the turkey breast is cooked through, remove, shred and return to pot.

7. Add the remaining cranberries and serve.

tip

This soup can be made a day in advance and heated up in the morning. If you do not have fresh cranberries, you can use dried ones and soak them in water for 30 minutes to rehydrate them before using.

SOUPE DE CÉLÉRI ET CHÂTAIGNE
(CELERY ROOT & CHESTNUT SOUP)
SERVES 4-6

You know by now that I love chestnuts, so it's no surprise that I have been experimenting with them, and mixing them with other ingredients. This is one combo that is definitely working! Is is comforting, hearty, and simply delicious.

2 tbsp olive oil

4 large shallots, minced

Salt and pepper

2 lb celery root, peeled and cut into 1/2-inch pieces

1 potato, peeled and diced

1 jar (15 oz.) store-bought steamed peeled chestnuts

6 cups vegetable stock

1 tbsp fresh lemon juice

Fresh thyme leaves for garnish

1. Gently heat the olive oil in a large, heavy saucepan.

2. Add the shallots and a generous pinch of salt and cook over moderate heat, stirring, until the shallots are softened and just starting to brown, about 5 minutes.

3. Stir in the celery root and potato and cook until the celery just starts to soften, about 5 minutes.

4. Add the chestnuts and the stock, bring to a simmer, cover and simmer for 30 minutes.

5. Working in batches, purée the soup in a blender.

6. Return the soup to the saucepan and warm over low heat. Stir in the lemon juice and season with salt.

7. Ladle the soup into bowls, garnish with thyme leaves and serve.

Tip

Adding mushrooms to this recipe would make it taste even more amazing.

If you prefer a lighter soup, you can remove the potato from the recipe.

PLAT PRINCIPAL (MAIN COURSE)

Pumpkin Risotto

Pork Tenderloin

Chicken with Nutty Creme Sauce

Tomato Tartin

Winter Vegetable Pot Pie

Stuffed Chicken

RISOTTO AU POTIRON
(PUMPKIN RISOTTO)
SERVES 6

Italian food is a part of my heritage, I love its variety and simplicity at the same time. Risotto is always a crowd-pleaser and much easier to prepare than you may think. This is one of my favorite dishes to serve to a lot of people. Pumpkin and risotto together scream: *holidays!*

5-6 cups vegetable stock

2 tbsp olive oil

1 medium white onion, chopped

3/4 cup dry wine

1 1/2 tsp freshly grated nutmeg

1 tsp freshly ground white pepper

1 tsp salt

1 1/2 cups Arborio rice

1 1/2 cups pumpkin purée

1/2 cup freshly grated Parmesan cheese, plus more for serving

1/2 cup pecans, lightly toasted

There are two ways to do this, on the stove or in the oven. I tend to favor the first one; it is a bit more work but the extra time allows for more flavor to emerge.

Option One

1. In a medium saucepan, bring the vegetable stock to a boil over medium heat. Reduce the heat to low and keep the stock hot.

2. In a medium saucepan, heat 2 tbsp olive oil over medium heat and add the onion. Add the rice and cook over medium heat, stirring with a wooden spoon, until the onions are translucent, about 3 minutes.

3. Add the wine and stir for another minute.

4. Immediately stir in 1 cup of the hot stock and cook, stirring constantly, until all of the liquid has been absorbed, about 2 minutes.

5. Reduce the heat to medium-low and gradually add 3 more cups of the hot stock, 1 cup at a time, stirring and cooking until each cup is almost absorbed before adding the next, about 15 minutes.

6. Stir in the pumpkin purée. Continue adding the remaining 2 cups stock, 1 cup at a time, stirring and cooking as above, until the rice is tender, about 10 minutes longer. The risotto should be creamy.

7. Spoon the risotto into 6 warmed soup plates and sprinkle the Parmesan and the pecans on top, and serve immediately

Option Two

1. Preheat oven to 425 degrees F.

2. In a Dutch oven (cooking pot), heat the oil over medium-high heat.

3. Add the onion and cook, stirring, until translucent, 2-3 minutes.

4. Add the rice and cook, stirring to coat the grains with oil, about 1 minute.

5. Stir in the wine and cook until it has completely evaporated, about 1 minute.

6. Stir in 4 cups of the stock, salt, and pepper. Bring to a boil.

7. Cover, transfer to the oven, and bake until most of the liquid has been absorbed by the rice, 20 to 25 minutes. You may need to check half way and add more stock.

8. Remove from oven, stir in 1/2 to 3/4 cup additional stock and the pumpkin purée. The risotto should be creamy.

10. Sprinkle with cheese. Garnish with pecans and serve immediately.

RÔTI DE PORC AUX LÉGUMES
(ROASTED PORK TENDERLOIN WITH APPLES)
SERVES 6

This is easy to assemble and prepare, and makes a nice alternative to turkey or roast beef, which are so often served during the Holidays. When the veggies cook together with the meat, all the flavors combine beautifully. Who doesn't love a one-pot dish?

2 tbsp grapeseed oil

1 2-lb boneless center cut pork loin, trimmed and tied

1 medium onion, sliced

2 carrots, sliced

1 fennel bulb, greens removed, trimmed and sliced

3 sprigs fresh thyme

2 apples, peeled, cored and sliced

2 tbsp apple cider vinegar

2 tbsp whole grain mustard

Salt & pepper

1. Preheat the oven to 400 degrees F.

2. In a large Dutch oven, heat the vegetable oil over high heat.

3. Season the pork loin generously all over with salt and pepper. Coat with all of the mustard.

4. Sear the meat until golden brown on all sides, about 2 to 3 minutes per side. Transfer to a plate and set aside.

5. Add the onion, carrot, garlic, and herb sprigs to the dutch oven. Stir until the vegetables are browned, about 8 minutes.

6. Add the apple cider vinegar and let it reduce, stirring, for another 2 minutes.

7. Add the apples and place the pork loin back in.

8. Transfer the Dutch oven to the preheated oven and roast until cooked through, 30-35 minutes.

9. Slice and serve on a platter, surround with the veggies and apples, and pour on the sauce.

tip
Use your leftover pork to make a sandwich the next day - just add some extra dijon mustard!

POULET EN ROBE D'AUTOMNE
(CHICKEN WITH A NUTTY CREAMY SAUCE)
SERVES 4-6

This recipe is based on my Mom's recipe for pheasant. She would prepare it during pheasant season in the fall and it was one of my favorite holiday meals. I make the dish every year, but since pheasant is quite delicate and can be scary to prepare, as well as difficult to find, I came up with this chicken version. It's much easier. Turkey would also taste excellent with this sauce.

4 chicken breasts, bone and skin on

salt & pepper

1 tsp thyme, divided

1 tbsp olive oil

1/2 cup plus 2 tbsp chicken stock

1/4 cup cranberry sauce (pg. 32)

1/2 cup roasted pine nuts (also delicious with walnuts)

3/4 cup white seedless grapes, cut in half

1/2 cup half & half

For the sauce

1/4 cup of cranberry sauce (pg. 32)

1/2 cup of roasted pine nuts (also delicious with walnuts)

3/4 cup of white seedless grapes cut in half

1/2 cup of chicken stock

1/2 cup of half and half

salt & pepper

1. Preheat the oven to 350 degrees F. Place chicken breasts in a shallow flame-proof baking dish, skin side up. Add 2 tbsp chicken stock.

2. Sprinkle each breast with salt, pepper and half the thyme.

3. Brush with olive oil and roast for 1 hour or until done. Transfer to a plate and cover with foil while you make the sauce.

4. Place the chicken stock in the dish you used to bake the chicken and heat gently, scraping the bottom with a wooden spoon. This way you will get all the chicken residue into the sauce.

5. Stir or whisk in the cream and bring to a gentle simmer.

6. Add the pine nuts, cranberry sauce, grapes, and salt and pepper and combine well.

7. Remove the skin and bones from the chicken breasts and slice.

Tip

Drizzle the sauce on any of the purées on pages x, they go so well together.

TARTE TATIN AUX TOMATES
(Tomato Tarte Tatin with Caramalized Onions)
Serves 8

A tarte tatin is usually prepared with apples or pears as a dessert. It is very French, sort of the European equivalent of the American Apple Pie. I ate countless tartes tatins growing up. One day in California I thought, why not try a tarte tatin with tomatoes? The result was a huge success. My boys, who swear that they don't like tomatoes, love this dish! Even in winter, when tomatoes are not in season but you can still find plum tomatoes, the dish works, because the tomatoes are cooked down and sweetened.

2 tbsp olive oil, plus additional for the pan

1 large onion

1 tsp cane sugar

8 large plum tomatoes, cut in half

3 tbsp unsalted butter at room temperature

1/3 cup maple syrup

1 sheet frozen puff pastry, thawed

Egg wash made with 1 egg beaten with 1 tablespoon water

A few fresh thyme sprigs

1. Heat 1 tbsp olive oil in a large skillet over medium heat and cook the onion for about 10 minutes, stirring often, until beautifully golden. Stir in sugar and cook for another couple of minutes. Transfer the onion and juices to a bowl and set aside.

2. Preheat oven to 425 degrees F.

3. Drizzle olive oil over bottom of a 9-inch, 2- to 3-inch-deep ovenproof skillet (preferably cast iron).

4. Mix 1/3 cup of maple syrup with 1 tbsp of olive oil and pour into the skillet. Arrange tomato halves, rounded side down and close together, in concentric circles in the skillet to fill completely.

5. Cover with the puff pastry and brush with egg wash. This will give a nice brown, flaky crust.

6. Place skillet in oven and bake tart 35-40 minutes. Let it cool for 10 minutes and cut around sides of skillet to loosen pastry.

7. Place large platter over skillet. Using oven mitts, hold skillet and platter firmly together and invert, allowing tart to settle onto platter.

Serve warm or at room temperature.

tip

You can assemble the dish a day in advance and pop into the oven when ready to serve.

VOL AU VENT VÉGÉTARIEN
(Winter Vegetable Pot Pie)
Serves 6

A warm and comforting traditional Belgian dish, perfect for the long and cold winters we have there. It may look scary when you see the list of ingredients, but the beauty of this potpie is that you can use whatever veggies you like, making it your own personal recipe. With all the farmers markets , this is so much fun!

You will need approximately 5-6 cups of chopped veggies.

Here are the ones I used for this recipe:

1 large parsnip, peeled and chopped

1 1/2 cups peeled and cubed butternut squash

1 large sweet potato, peeled and cubed

1.5 tbsp olive oil

1/2 yellow onion, diced

1/2 leek, thinly sliced

2 carrots, peeled and diced

8 oz mushrooms, sliced

1/2 cup flour

1 quart vegetable broth

1 tsp salt

1/2 tsp pepper

1 tsp oregano

1/4 cup half and half

1 box defrosted puff pastry

1 egg, lightly beaten (add water or milk and whisk to it to make egg wash)

1. Bring a large pot of water to a boil. Add the parsnip, butternut squash and sweet potato cubes and simmer until just tender—about 10-15 minutes. Drain and set veggies aside.

2. In another large pot, heat the olive oil over medium heat. Add the onion and leeks and sauté for about 5 minutes, until tender. Add the carrots and mushrooms and continue to cook for another 10 minutes, until carrots are tender. Sprinkle with the flour and mix until combined.

3. Add the vegetable stock, salt, pepper, oregano and Half & Half, and bring mixture to a boil, stirring continuously until very thick. Add cooked root veggies to the pot and season additionally to taste.

4. Preheat oven to 425 degrees F.

5. Roll out the dough on a floured surface, Cut it into six 8-inch rounds. Fill the ramekins with the vegetable mixture and cover with the dough, folding the edges of the crusts over the ramekins. Crimp the edges (may need to use some egg wash as glue, so the dough will stick the ramekin). Brush the egg wash over the top of the puff pastry. Make 2 slits in the top of each with a paring knife than season the top crusts with flakey salt and freshly ground black pepper.

6. Arrange the ramekins on a rimmed baking sheet and place in the oven for 15 minutes. Turn the oven down to 375 degrees F, and continue baking for an hour, until golden.

tip

To create variations of this recipe you can add chicken, turkey, or lobster. Even turkey meatballs would be good with this!

POULET FARCI
(Stuffed Chicken)
Serves 5

I think stuffing is my favorite part of the Holiday meal. So I thought why not come up with a version that is so easy to prepare that I can do it any time, something that is also a bit lighter than a regular stuffing so I do not feel too guilty eating it so often. The fun part with this is that you can have fun with the ingredients and mix and match them so you never get tired of the dish.

1 tbsp olive oil, plus more for drizzling

1 small onion, chopped

1 celery stalk, chopped

1 garlic clove, minced

1/2 cup chopped jarred chestnuts

2 tbsp butter, divided

Salt & pepper

1/2 tsp chopped fresh thyme

8 4-oz.boneless skinless chicken breast halves, pounded

1. Preheat the oven to 350 degrees F.
2. Heat 1 tbsp oil over medium heat in a small nonstick skillet and sauté the onion, celery and garlic until tender. Season with salt and pepper and add the thyme.
3. Add the chestnuts and sauté for another 2-3 minutes.
4. Flatten the chicken and sprinkle with salt and pepper.
5. Spread the vegetables over the flattened chicken breasts and roll up in a pinwheel. Secure with either string or toothpicks. Place in a baking dish and drizzle with olive oil.
6. Bake, uncovered for 35-40 minutes.

tip

You can make the stuffing in advance and store it in the fridge for 2-3 days.

DESSERTS (DESSERTS)

Cafe Liégois

Eggnog Panna Cotta

Chocolat Pot de Creme

Warm Scandinavian Wine

Roasted Apples with Speculoos

Poached Pears

Orange Nut Cake

Homemade Eggnog

Eggnog Ice Cream

CAFÉ LIÉGOIS
(COFFEE ICE CREAM SUNDAY)
SERVES 6

Café Liégeois is a cold dessert with origins in the city of Lièges, which is located in the southerneast part of Belgium. It generally consists of two scoops of coffee ice cream and one scoop of vanilla ice cream, together with chantilly (whipped) cream and coffee. Usually you serve it with cold coffee, but I have made it with hot coffee as well and it is a nice twist on an Afogatto, which is an Italian version of the dessert. Nothing is better than eating ice cream with the ones you love!

1 pint of your favorite coffee ice cream

1 pint of your favorite vanilla ice cream

2 cups coffee (hot or cold, your choice)

whipped cream

coffee beans

1. Scoop the icecream into 6 ramekins or small bowls
2. Pour 1/3 cup of coffee over each, add whipped cream and sprinkle some crushed coffee beans on top.
3. Voila!

tip
Try using cappuccino chip ice cream or chocolate ice cream.

EGGNOG PANNA COTTA
(EGGNOG PANNA COTTA)
SERVES 6

Panna Cotta takes me back to my memories of vacations with my dad in Italy. I have always loved this dessert. It is just sweet enough, you can embellish it with fresh fruit or sauces, and you can make it with so many different flavors: vanilla, chocolate, strawberry, even basil … I love cooking this way, following my tastes buds where they want to go, exploring and mixing flavors! The dessert may seem intimidating, but in fact it is one of the easiest desserts ever. The eggnog makes this version particularly festive!

1/4 ounce gelatin (from 1 packet)
1/4 cup cold milk
2 3/4 cups cold eggnog
Freshly grated nutmeg or cinnamon, for serving

1. Sprinkle gelatin over milk; let stand to soften.
2. Heat 3/4 cup eggnog in a saucepan until bubbles appear on the edges. Remove from the heat and stir in gelatin mixture, then the remaining 2 cups eggnog. Divide among six 6-ounce ramekins.
3. Chill in the fridge for 3-4 hours, until set.
4. Dip the bottoms of ramekins into a bowl of hot water for 15 seconds. Run a knife around sides and unmold onto plates.
5. Serve, sprinkled with nutmeg or cinnamon, and maybe even drizzle with maple syrup or honey. The panna cotta can be made up to 2 days in advance and removed from their molds right before serving.

POT DE CRÈME AU CHOCOLAT
(MINI CHOCOLATE PUDDINGS)
SERVES 6

These are best served in single-serving dishes. They are perfect for a gathering of friends. I find that when I serve these there's a moment of silence during the first few bites. Chocolate can have that effect! My recipe uses coconut milk because I love the flavor of chocolate and coconut together, but this recipe will work perfectly with regular, soy, or almond milk as well.

1 egg

¼ cup maple syrup

1 1/2 tsp instant espresso powder

1 1/2 tsp organic vanilla extract

8 oz chopped unsweetened chocolate

1 cup coconut milk

1. Place all of the ingredients except the milk in a Vitamix or powerful blender.
2. Heat the coconut milk in a small saucepan until very hot, but take it off the heat before it reaches a boil.
3. With the blender running on low, slowly and carefully pour in the hot coconut milk.
4. Blend together until the chocolate is completely melted, and the mixture is smooth and thick.
5. Pour the mixture into serving cups and refrigerate until set, about 2 hours.

tip
Once the mixture is set, the chocolate pots can stay in the fridge and will keep for up to 2 days.

VIN CHAUD SCANDINAVE
(Warm Scandinavian Wine)
Serves 6-8

This drink reminds me of my time in college in Brussels. Every December we would drink this warm, sweet wine full of nuts and a touch of cinnamon. When the weather was cold and we had to study, this was a great end to the day! Enjoy this in moderation, it is surprisingly strong.

1 bottle red wine

1 cinnamon stick

1/2 cup orange juice

2 orange peels

1/4 cup maple syrup

1/2 cup fresh cranberries

1/2 tsp of ground cloves

1 cup nuts (optional)

1. Place everything in a sauce pan, stir together and place over high heat. Let the mixture reduce for

20 minutes, covered, so all the flavors combine nicely together.

2. Divide evenly into cups and enjoy!

Tip
For an additional flavor touch, add a stick of cinnamon to your mixture.

POMME AU FOUR AVEC SPECULOOS
(ROASTED APPLES WITH SPECULOOS CRUMBS & VANILLA ICE CREAM)
SERVES 4

Speculoos (also called biscof) is a traditional Belgian coffee cookie. I grew up eating them in every way you can imagine: dunked in milk, in a sandwich, with marshmallows for s'mores, crumbled onto ice cream or yogurt... The mix of the ice cream with the crumbled cookies gives these baked apples a revolutionary twist.

6 apples (Honeycrisp, Jonagold or Golden are my favorites for this recipe)
1/2 cup chopped pecans
3 tbsp maple syrup or coconut sugar
1 tsp cinnamon
pinch of salt
vanilla ice cream

1. Preheat the oven to 350 degrees F. Rinse and dry the apples and cut out the cores, leaving the bottom 1/2 inch of the apples intact.

2. Combine the pecans, maple syrup (or coconut sugar), cinnamon and salt and stuff the apples. Transfer to a baking dish.

3. Bake in the preheated oven for 30 to 45 minutes, depending on the apple you are using, until tender.

4. Serve warm, topped with vanilla ice cream and crumbled speculoos. The mix of the warm cinnamon apple, with the smoothness of the ice cream and the crunchiness of the speculoos is just divine!

POIRES POCHÉES
(Poached Pears)
Serves 6

These are really easy to prepare, yet they make a chic dessert! You can prepare the pears in advance and serve them at room temperature, or warm them up before serving.

4 firm, medium-size pears, peeled

1 bottle red wine

1/3 cup maple syrup

1 tsp pure vanilla extract

1 whole cinnamon stick

1 strip orange peel

1 strip lemon peel

1/4 tsp ground cloves

1. Place the pears in medium saucepan.

2. Add the remaining ingredients and add just enough water to cover pears.

3. Set saucepan over high heat, and bring liquid to a boil.

4. Reduce to a simmer and cook gently over medium-low heat, stirring occasionally, until a paring knife easily pierces the pears, about 15 minutes.

5. Remove from heat and allow pears to cool in the liquid.

6. Transfer the pears to a plate.

7. Discard the solids, and return liquid to medium-high heat. Bring to a boil and cook until liquid has been reduced to a syrup, about 45 minutes. Remove from heat and allow to cool.

8. Store pears in an airtight container until ready to serve. To serve, arrange pears on plates and serve with or without the wine syrup. This dish goes well with vanilla ice cream, and can also be used as a pie filling.

tip

When ready to serve, arrange pears on plates and serve with or without liquid. This dish goes well with vanilla ice cream, and can also be used as the fruits for a pie filling.

GATEAU AUX ORANGES ET AUX AMANDES
(Orange Nut Cake)
Serves 4-6

You will not believe how easy is to prepare this cake until you've tried it. For those who are not super confident about baking, this is almost impossible to mess up! It is a friendly food that can be served for breakfast, snack or dessert. This will become your go-to baking item, and might even become your holiday favorite!

1/2 cup whole wheat or all-purpose flour

1 cup nuts (any kind you like, I used almonds here and have tried pistachios, yum!)

1 1/2 tsp baking powder

1/2 tsp salt

3 eggs

1/2 cup olive oil

1/2 cup maple syrup

1/2 tsp pure vanilla extract

Zest of 1 orange

1/4 cup orange juice

1. Preheat your oven to 350F, grease a 9 inch cake pan or mini bundt cakes pan.
2. Whisk together the flour, baking powder, salt, vanilla and nuts.
3. Separately, beat together the eggs, olive oil, and maple syrup. Add the vanilla, orange juice and orange zest.
4. Combine the wet mix with the dry ingredients. Scrape into the prepared pan.
5. Bake at 25-30 minutes until the cake is golden brown and a tester comes out clean.

tip
If serving as a dessert, try adding some whipped cream or vanilla ice cream.

CRÈME GLACÉE AU LAIT DE POULE
(EGGNOG ICE CREAM)
SERVES 4-6

1 quart store-bought or homemade eggnog

1. Divide the eggnog evenly between 2 ice-cube trays.

2. Freeze until solid, 3-4 hours. The ice cubes can be made up to a week in advance, just transfer to a zip lock bag. Do not leave exposed or it will compromise the taste.

3. Put as many cubes as you wish to make ice cream in a food processor and pulse. Let the processor run for a little while until you get a smooth, gelato-like consistency.

4. Scoop the ice cream into bowls and serve.

5. Top with Biscoff (Speculoos) crumbs! The best!

HOMEMADE EGGNOG

2 eggs

1/2 tsp cinnamon

1/4 cup agave nector or maple syrup

1 1/2 cups regular milk

1 tsp vanilla extract

1. Put everything in the blender and blend until smooth, about 30 seconds to 1 minute depending on the strength of your blender.

tips

Try adding a tsp of tumeric to give the eggnog a warm, exotic flavor.

Substitute the regular milk for almond milk for a vegan version.

To make an adult version, add 3 oz. of rum to the mixture before blending.

Merci Beaucoup!

Virginie Degryse lives in Los Angeles, California with her
husband Laurent, their kids Marine, 12, Charlie, 10, Harry, 7,
and their two dogs Sandy and Benji.
She is the author of the Crave and Cook Food blog
www.craveandcook.com
Follow her on Instagram
@craveandcook
Share your photos with
#craveandcook
and keep in touch.
virginie@craveandcook.com

INDEX

INDEX

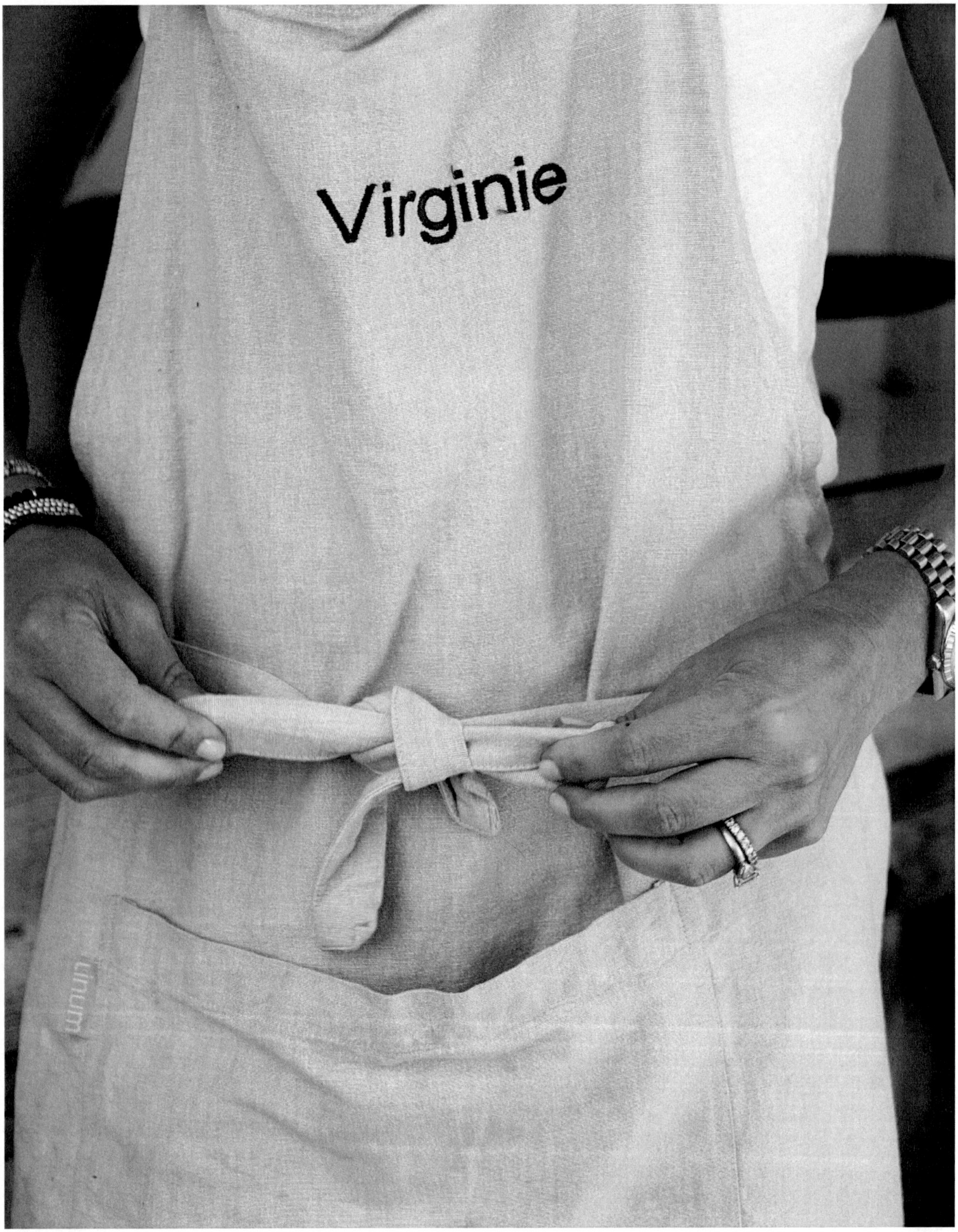
Virginie
linum

WWW.CRAVEANDCOOK.COM

CRAVE
AND
COOK

Virginie Degryse

43263781R00065

Made in the USA
San Bernardino, CA
16 December 2016